HEAVEN SENT

MY FAMILY'S REMARKABLE

ENCOUNTER WITH THE

VIRGIN MARY

James P. Naughton

Key Publishing Company

ISBN 978-0-9858377-3-0
HEAVEN SENT

Key Publishing Company

www.KeyPublishingCompany.com
51 Gosnold Road
North Kingstown, RI 02852

401-486-9601
jnaughton60@gmail.com

Printed in the U.S.A.

Editing, design, and layout by
Kip Williams Design

I dedicate this book to my cousin Jack Hughes
who is truly "Heaven Sent"

INTRODUCTION

I realize that I have waited a long time—twenty-five-plus years—to tell this story; however, it took me fifty-plus years to publish my most recent book, *Whatever Happened to the Pecords?* in 2014. I guess I just sit on things and mull them over for years. In fairness, I didn't have time for writing until I retired in 2008.

The decision to share my family's supernatural encounter with a crying statue of the Virgin Mary at a church in Virginia was for many reasons difficult to make. I could imagine the effect and skepticism from my children's classmates and also from friends of my wife Sharon's and mine if I wrote it back then.

At the time, we naïvely felt that this was a private event for us, the parishioners and few other tourists. We did not discuss it very often among ourselves. I believe that to witness a supernatural event like we did has profound effects on one's life forever. As parents, we trust that it is a positive one for our children. In this book, I do discuss one change in my daughter Erin, who was 14 at the time, and her subsequent correspondence with the parish priest.

My intention in writing now is to let those who are traveling to Our Lady of Guadalupe Church in Hobbs, New Mexico know that Mary has been making her

ii   **James Naughton**

presence known for hundreds of years all over the world. It's not haphazard: There is always a reason for her apparitions and her crying statues. If you go, prepare yourself for a miracle. My thought from our experience twenty-five years ago was "We are definitely not "alone," and we are being watched over by Mother Mary."

Heaven-sent proof!

Have you seen the news articles and pictures referring to a statue of Mother Mary crying? This time it's happening in New Mexico (see picture on back cover).

It seems that sometimes she speaks to chosen individuals, as she did to the children of Fatima, Portugal, in 1917, and Medjugorje, in 1981. Sometimes she sheds tears as she is doing now in New Mexico or leaves a sign, such as the miraculous painting of herself as Our Lady of Guadalupe on the inside of Juan Diego's cape in Mexico in 1531. That happened ten years after the Spanish put an end to the Aztecs' bloody human sacrifices, and at the time there were very few converts to Catholicism: only 400.

By 1541, ten years after the miracle in Guadalupe, ten million people of Mexico had converted to Catholicism! I believe she knows that many will require proof, so she usually provides it. At Fatima, she performed the "miracle of the sun" in front of thousands.

I also believe that her apparitions are not haphazard—meaning that there are specific reasons for them. Just study their history.

In some cases they are warnings of future events. A frightening example of this is portrayed in the book

Our Lady of Kibeho (in the heart of Africa) by Immaculee Ilibagiza. In 1981, the Virgin Mary appeared to eight young people. Over the next few years she gave warnings of a possible Holocaust in Rwanda. Sadly, her messages were ignored by government officials, and in 1994 genocide swept across Rwanda and left more than a million dead!

Maybe this time it's because of the proximity to Mexico and the border. Maybe she is broken-hearted and crying for the babies being ripped from the mothers. She is after all, Mother Mary, mother of Jesus Christ and, for believers, the mother of the whole world.

From everything I have read of her apparitions and "crying statues," she hasn't asked for a lot: just prayer and a request for us to say the Rosary.

If you think about it, her SON, who brutally died on the cross for us, never asked a lot of us either; mostly "obey the commandments, and be kind to the least of my brethren." Sounds too simple, but it's true!

But who am I to try and explain the phenomenon and the miracles taking place today and throughout history? I am no saint, and I still struggle to understand like many. I'm just a husband, a father, and a grandfather, who, along with his family, stumbled onto what appeared to us to be a miracle—a supernatural event.

What I am about to share with you, I have only shared with very close family members. I always thought I didn't have permission to discuss it. I am still questioning. The feeling that it was time to share came over me soon after reading about the events at Our Lady of Guadalupe Catholic Church, Hobbs, New Mexico.

Why now? I think reading the multiple news articles about the supernatural events occurring at the church in New Mexico stirred up memories my family mostly have only discussed among ourselves. Memories that we are still coming to grips with twenty-five years later. Maybe our experience will help parishioners in New Mexico and other locations understand that this is not the first time that SHE has made her presence known. It's my opinion that Mary, comes at particular and chosen times for more than one mission.

In April of 1992 we were returning from what my kids considered our last "Chevy Chase road trip" ("Wally World") to Disney World in Orlando, Florida—last because Timmy, our oldest, would be heading off to college in September, and we had been making these trips each Spring vacation since 1982. My job entailed a lot of travel, so I enjoyed the two-day road trip as a chance to bond with my kids. I loved it and miss it: the fighting, the yelling, and all. I was fortunate to be able to travel the world, but Disneyland was my wife Sharon's and my favorite destination, and this was also true with my kids.

Now on our way home, Easter Week, 1992, I spontaneously decided upon reaching the South Carolina border to take a couple of hours and drive over to Parris Island, where I attended boot camp many years ago. I facetiously told Tim that I was going to show him the alternative to not doing well in college. As we drove across the bridge from Beaufort, South Carolina, I pointed to the vast swamp that separated the island from the mainland... no way out.

We got permission to drive into 3rd Battalion, my former battalion, nicknamed coincidentally and sarcastically Disneyland, because it was newer and of brick construction, vs the older 1st and 2nd Battalions that were metal Quonset huts and wooden buildings.

Our timing was great, because the recruits were in the middle of bayonet practice and the drill instructors were roughhousing with them a bit. Tim said, "They're just putting on a show because of us tourists." I had to inform him that it was the other way around: They were being extra nice because of us tourists. Point made.

We ended up staying the night in Savannah and headed out the next morning for our destination, Washington, DC. As we entered Virginia, there were plenty of roadside advertisements for King's Dominion Amusement Park.

After all these years I can still hear their voices: "Can we go, please, please can we go?" "They have the best roller coaster!" they continued.

Well, we figured, this might be the last such road trip, and it was on our side of the highway, so we relented. Once in the park, they headed straight for the roller coaster. They were literally just belted in when the first thunder and lightning struck. The ride never started and everyone was escorted off. Almost immediately, we heard an announcement that the entire park was shutting down. Unreal, I thought.

Within 10 mins we were back in our car with "rain checks" instead of cash back. Unbelievable. *Are you kidding me?* Later on, I believe you will find that this was a little more than a coincidence.

I was also a little irritated that I let myself get "conned" into stopping and paying for some expensive tickets after spending a pretty good penny at Disney World and then having this happen.

OK! So: We continued toward DC. The car radio announcer mentioned Holy Saturday and I instantly thought, "Let's go to Mass." Then I said it out loud and was greeted with "No! Do we have to?"

Ignoring their complaints, I asked Sharon to rummage through the glove compartment for a *USA Today* newspaper that I threw in on the way down. (While spending the night at a hotel, I'd noticed an article in the paper discussing a statue of Mary that was crying human tears at a church in Virginia. I'd planned on reading it when we got to Orlando, but never did.)

Next, I asked if she could find the name of the town mentioned in the article. She said, "It was Lakeridge." I pulled off the highway at the next road stop to look at our map. I could not find Lakeridge anywhere.

I used my company car phone (In the early 90s, it was a Panasonic, the size of a shoe box.) and called Triple A. The attendant informed me that Lakeridge was actually a village in the town of Woodbridge 25 miles south of DC and only about 20 minutes from where we were. I was beginning to believe we needed to go to this church. Virginia is a big state and Lakeridge could have been hours away. It also crossed my mind that if it hadn't been for that thunderstorm, we'd still be at King's Dominion. I decided it was meant to be.

We got off at the Woodbridge exit and pulled into a 7-11 where we were directed into Lakeridge and St. Elizabeth Anne Seton Catholic Church. I notice that all the homes seemed similar—two story beautiful colonials with lush landscaping. I remember thinking "This is definitely an affluent neighborhood, and most apparitions and supernatural events that I'm familiar with seemed to occur in poorer areas."

We could see a church and parking lot located in a heavily populated pine tree section of the neighborhood. It seemed as though the church was built especially for them. It had the look of a building you might find in the deep woods of Maine or Vermont.

We parked and all got out of our van about the same time as two other cars showed up. An Asian couple was already taking pictures. As everyone— approximately ten tourists—approached the church entrance, a woman who looked like a nun, dressed in a white high-neck blouse and black long skirt, came out and began admonishing everyone that this was private property and suggesting we leave the premises. I instantly copped an attitude and turned around and headed back to the van. Sharon and the kids remained.

Looking back for them, I saw a young man step out onto the porch. He had on a pair of jeans and a red plaid shirt. He reminded me of a Hollywood actor with blonde hair and a mustache. "Maybe he's a musician for the church choir," I thought.

When he asked why they were leaving, they told him that they were asked to. He then said, "You are all welcome," and pleaded with them not to leave. He also told them his name was Father James Bruse. Sharon began waving to me to come back, which I reluctantly started to do.

As I got close, I heard one of the tourists ask "Are you the bleeding priest?" He began to simultaneously raise his arms while rolling down his sleeves, exposing crusted wounds on both wrists. We all stared with eyes wide open. Finally, I blurted out, "Father what's going on?"

He nonchalantly explained that he was saying Mass on Christmas Eve, and when it came to the Offertory portion of the service, he (as customary) raised the Host with both hands and noticed, along with the congregation, that blood was spilling down his arms onto his vestments.

At first he said that he thought that he had cut himself on the corner of the stone altar. He then recalled sitting down and feeling a stinging pain in his side.

When he looked down he saw blood seeping through the garment. Some in attendance began to rush up to the altar to try and help him. He then said his feet began to feel soaking wet. When he looked down, he realized they were bleeding.

He confirmed he knew then that he had what is known as Stigmata: "The Wounds of Christ." After that, any time he was near a statue, it began to shed tears.

Without thinking, I said, "Father, my wife is slowly losing her eyesight. Would you say a prayer for her?" He reached over and cupped her head in his hands and prayed. I can't imagine what the crowd was thinking. (I will discuss Sharon's affliction and the miraculous outcome later on).

It might sound brazen, but without skipping a beat, I then asked if he would mind if I went into the church to say a prayer. Holy Saturday Mass was to begin in about twenty minutes. He said, "Sure, go ahead."

I nervously walked in, blessed myself by making the sign of the cross at the holy water font at the front of the church, and walked down the center aisle toward the sanctuary. I noted how different and beautiful it looked. It appeared larger than it seemed on the outside and reminded me, as I intimated earlier, of a cabin in northern New England with a spiritual ambience.

Inside the sanctuary railing was a brown five-foot wooden statue of the Blessed Mother. I was all alone at this point and I wondered: was this the "crying" statue mentioned in the *USA Today* article? I stood there and began to silently recite the Hail Mary. Suddenly, I heard a slap on the floor in front of me. It seemed like it was a splash of water that I assumed came from a pipe overhead. However, there wasn't any pipe that I could see.

I returned my gaze to the statue and began to recall some of the comments by cynics who proclaimed the tears were most likely moisture caused by air-conditioning, etc. but it was April, and I didn't think the air conditioners would have been on then. Astonishingly, I saw what appeared to be a tear welling up on the corner of her left eye. In awe I watched it grow bigger and travel across her eye to the right and stream down the middle of the statue. This was followed by another and another. I looked around and felt like Doubting Thomas.

I felt compelled to go behind the railing and the statue to, I guess, make sure there wasn't a hose or something hooked up to it. There wasn't.

I began to feel a little weak and decided to sit down in a front pew a little to the left of her. I kept reciting the Hail Mary and became extremely nervous. I wondered: *Is this really happening? Why?*

Timmy, my eldest, 18, was the first to come in and he walked right down to the statue, followed by Matthew, 16, Erin, 14, and then Sharon. Sharon sat down next to me in the pew and asked what was happening. The parishioners now were beginning to stream in as well. I notice Timmy's face looked ashen white and he waved to me to come over. I practically ran. He said "Dad, I think she is talking to us."

I have to admit I was scared. My mind was racing. I realized that she was crying so hard that her lips seemed to be quivering. (I learned later that the human bottom lip is controlled by the parasympathetic nervous system, which also controls the tear ducts.) I immediately and ever since began using the word "pursed" to describe the face of the statue, meaning in addition to quivering, her lips seemed to purse up similarly to a baby's. I'd never uttered that word in my life, previously.

Instinctively, and without thinking, I reached into my pocket, pulled out my handkerchief, and began to wipe the tears off her knee, which was as high as I could reach. (This produced a miracle, which I will discuss later.)

I suggested that the kids take a seat, as church caretakers were carrying out towels to soak up the tears. Evidently, they'd had some prior experience. Some began to cordon off the area around the statue with temporary felt railings, so no one would step on the soaking towels. The tears seemed to come quickly, creating a huge puddle.

A parishioner walked over and said, "Something, isn't it?"

I asked him the same question. "What is going on here?" I was thinking, *this isn't some famous cathedral, and we're in a relatively small village. How unusual for a neighborhood to have its own church right in the middle of it.*

He began telling me that his 12-year-old daughter attended the adjacent Catholic grammar school and the other day, while she and some classmates were in the foyer of the school, a statue in the corner began to cry. She told him the sister exclaimed "Oh, Father Bruse is probably in the area," and sure enough, the door opened, and it was Father Bruse.

He went on to say that it seems everywhere he goes, statues cry, and then he related another story: Apparently, an aunt of Father Bruse had passed on a few weeks earlier, and he went to a cathedral near Baltimore to say the funeral Mass. The parishioner and other members of the parish went to the service to support him. As Father Bruse began the service, he said, "All the paintings of saints in the cathedral's tall stained-glass windows started crying, and tears flooded the windows."

Mass was about to begin and we ended our conversation. I whispered to him, "Why? Why here?"

He quietly mentioned something about Father Bruse, a young extremely handsome man, questioning his vocation; whether or not to stay in the priesthood. I could understand. I had attended Catholic School in the 50s, and there was a lot of pressure to attend high school in a local seminary. A few of my classmates did, and a couple became priests. I know firsthand that it was not an easy decision for most of them. It just wasn't for me.

We shook hands and left for our seats. The thought kept reccurring: "Why was my family allowed to witness this miraculous event?" I figured it must have something to do with Sharon. She always had a spiritual side that was apparent to all that knew her. Not something she would wear on her sleeve, saying *look at me, look how holy I am*. Nothing like that: She just always had, and has, something. I was thinking maybe this experience had to do with her eye disease. She was due for an operation when we arrived home. (Another miracle regarding this happened when we got home. I will explain later.)

Father Bruse said Mass. His wounds did not open up even though we anticipated they would do so. I think we and the other tourists found it difficult to concentrate as the caretakers kept running back in forth picking up wet towels and replacing them with dry ones during the whole service.

We headed for DC to spend the night. No one said a word during the thirty-minute drive. We were all numb from the events of the day. As I was hanging up my slacks in the closet, I noticed my handkerchief protruding from the pocket. It was still a little damp, so I laid it near the window sill to dry. In the morning I placed it in a little plastic travel bag and left it in my suitcase. I didn't think about it again until we arrived home in Rhode Island.

***

The next day we toured around DC and spent some time at the Vietnam Wall. The kids were unusually quiet. Sharon had some high school friends from her hometown in Willimantic, Connecticut, whose names are etched on it and I had some as well, from my hometown of East Hartford, Connecticut.

I thought "We just left a mystery at St. Elizabeth Anne Seton Church in Lakeridge and now we're looking at this impressive, yet sad, wall." Over 50,000 young men and women: average age, 19! All are on this wall. Why? For what? To me, I'm sorry, it's also a mystery.

I was thinking "Why wasn't I on it? Fate? Luck? Or just not in my destiny?" I had joined the Marine Reserves in '63, right after President Kennedy was shot. I thought I would coordinate my obligation with College and possibly move to activate afterwards, but events put an end to that.

Sometimes I feel like one of those few people who walked away from a plane crash. It's hard to make sense out of life and its mysteries sometimes. I believed that I was meant to be there with my family, right then. Coincidence? I don't think so. ("Coincidences are God's way of remaining anonymous.")

We said goodbye to DC and headed home. Sharon and I said very little about what we considered a miracle at the church. I privately told her that I was convinced something bad was going to happen in our country (I will discuss my premonition further toward the end).

I found the kids very subdued during the ride back to Rhode Island. I think we were on the Jersey Turnpike when Tim asked, "Dad, do you think those were real tears?" At the time I didn't have a great answer. I just told him that I read that some university lab was analyzing a sample and we would have to wait until we arrive home. As it turned out, when the sample of her tears was analyzed, it was confirmed in the newspapers that they were human tears.

A day after we arrived home, I had a call from my boss who lives in Bar Harbor, Maine. He had some scientist friends who worked at the Bar Harbor Ocean Lab and were doing studies on sharks' eyes. He had, unbeknownst to me, taken the liberty to discuss Sharon's eye illness and her upcoming laser procedure in Rhode Island. They suggested that Sharon postpone the procedure until she was examined at Boston Eye and Ear by Dr. Clement Trempe, originally from Canada, a doctor and scientist who was one of the early inventors of the Eye Laser. They also confirmed that they would insure her getting an appointment.

What happened next is a story onto itself. For now, I will just say it was all a miracle. Dr. Trempe said that he confirmed that she had been invaded by a parasite that had maneuvered into her eye, and furthermore that if she had gone ahead with procedure in Rhode Island, it could have sealed it in permanently. He said that possibly it could have allowed it to penetrate her brain.

After two years of appointments with him in Boston, the sight in her good eye actually increased a little higher than 20/20 and the infected eye returned to 20/40. A miracle? We think so.

A week after we arrived home, vicious and violent race riots erupted in Los Angeles. One might recall the names: Rodney King and Reginald Denny. Their names were in the papers often in regards to those riots. I believed this was the warning—the premonition I mentioned earlier—and one of possibly a number of reasons, the statue was crying in the spring of 1992, during the celebration of her son's resurrection on Easter Sunday.

I somehow forgot to remove the plastic bag containing my handkerchief from the suitcase; however, I got a frantic call from my sister in Connecticut that her oldest boy (my nephew) was very ill with rheumatic fever. I instantly thought of my handkerchief and found and opened my travel bag.

There it was, in the plastic bag. When I opened it. I noticed something immediately. I called Sharon and we both stared in wonder at a rust-colored outline of

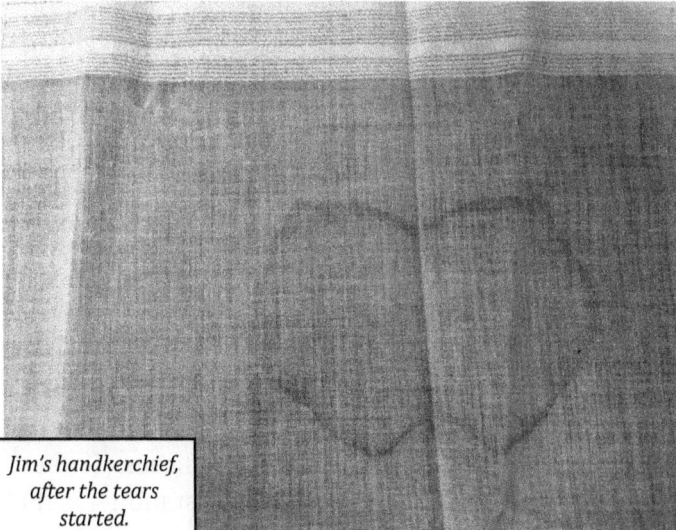

Jim's handkerchief, after the tears started.

a heart that appeared to have a small piece carved out near the bottom.

We called my sister and offered to bring it down, hoping that my nephew might benefit from Mother Mary's tears. He healed quickly and we believed it was another miracle.

As mentioned earlier I/we kept quiet about what happened and didn't let the handkerchief out of our house until a few years later. I loaned it to a friend for a family member and it provided no cure. We were upset for our friend and we began to question our right to be giving this holy cloth to anyone. We also thought the power might have dissipated.

In any event, we have kept it in a special place in our home along with the actual magazine article of the statue, Father Bruse, and the *USA Today* article, "Why Does Mother Mary Weep?" that I had stuffed in our van's glove compartment. We also enclosed some correspondence from Father Bruse, mainly between him and our daughter Erin.

Erin, who turned fourteen during our trip, was struggling in school at the time, so you can imagine how surprised we were that soon after we arrived home, she began writing poetry. She also wrote a poem of her impression of Father Bruse and the events at Lakeridge and mailed it to him. I will attach her poem and his reply at the end. A photo of the handkerchief—now fading—is on page 15.

One can Google a number of sites that discuss Father Bruse and the Crying Statue. My understanding is that it's typical that the Catholic Church sort of frowns on these type of supernatural happenings. They feel that one should believe because of faith, or because they say so.

I understand, as I think of Jesus' reply to his Apostle Thomas, when Thomas said he would believe (in the Resurrection) if he could place his fingers in Jesus' wounds. "Blessed art those who believe, but have not seen." As a human being, it's always nice to have a little "Heaven-sent proof" to boost your faith, I think.

About six years later, Sharon and I had an occasion to drive down to Washington, DC. Knowing we were only twenty or thirty minutes away from Lakeridge, Virginia, and St. Elizabeth Anne Seton church, we decided to drive down and check things out. We had no trouble finding our way, but were thoroughly surprised when we saw the church. Our little country church had been torn down and replaced by a huge modern church!

Once inside we noticed the wooden statue of Mary was gone, in fact after looking around, I could only find a tiny two inch by seven inch plaque about an inch from the floor in an obscure location noting that some events took place here in 1992. (Sorry, I misplaced my notes on the exact wording.) I could only assume that it was purposely hidden. I was a little depressed.

We met a caretaker outside who lives in the surrounding area. I asked about things. Was he around in 1992? He was. Where is Father Bruse? He said he was relocated out in the country towards the middle of Virginia and he is the pastor of a small country church.

Another miracle, I thought. *He decided to stay in the priesthood.*

Again, I don't know if that story about his questioning of faith and his vocation to the priesthood was true. Also, he wasn't sure if he still carried the Stigmata. I then asked if he, the caretaker, had been around when it all ended. He said that he was on his back deck barbecuing when all of a sudden it seemed as if heaven opened up and all kinds of lights, gold and other brilliant colors of some unknown substance started falling on him and his neighbors. That was it; that was the end of her presence.

That was the summer of 1992, I believe, although I am not one hundred percent certain of the date.

There have been many apparitions and signs of Mother Mary throughout history. I can certainly understand how many people are dismissive of supernatural events. I normally would be too, but not anymore.

And I can understand the clergy not wanting to embrace these events without absolute proof. When I read of the Mary statue in New Mexico crying a type of chrism tears, it brought up memories of Lakeridge.

And while I can't prove anything, I thought of our experience as sort of representing regular families. I thought by finally sharing, it might be helpful to anyone who is confused by such a supernatural event.

Also, in all fairness, I never wrote or published anything till after retirement in '08. I do not consider myself a great writer, but I have always been a good storyteller. Still, learning how to format and then publish it is a process.

As an aside, chrism I believe is olive oil that has been scented with a perfume. I also remember reading that Mary Magdalene used chrism when washing Jesus's feet with her hair.

As with Lakeridge and life in general, the crying statue in New Mexico is a mystery. Eventually, we will learn more as time goes on. It took many years before the world learned of the secrets in the letter given to the children of Fatima.

We know this as Christians: Mary and Jesus and Heaven would never condone shooting an unarmed young twenty-year-old girl from Honduras trying to seek asylum in our country, nor would they condone separating a three-year-old from her parents.

I hope Heaven knows that most of us abhor this awful situation and are praying for those poor souls who are trying to escape their dangerous environments and make better and safer lives for their children. I think, at the very least, she wants us to make our feelings known to our representatives. This isn't a matter of what political party one belongs to. I don't think she is calling for open borders, but rather it's a call for humanity and kindness "to the least of our brethren."

I know human nature. And I know readers will want to ask many questions such as, *How did the experience change your life* and *how did it affect your children's, etc., etc.?*

So I will leave a link to my book website *www.KeypublishingCompany.com* and my email at Key Publishing Company, *info@keypulishingcompany.com* and try to do the best that I can. I can just tell you that, yes, we experienced what we believed to be miracles related to our experience.

I will also tell you that we have had some private catastrophes. In other words, our experience at St. Elizabeth Anne church didn't protect or prevent us from experiencing life. We didn't win the lottery, nor should one think of it in terms of material wealth. It did add to our faith. If you think about it being here on earth, experiencing life is a miracle in and of itself. Not having bad experiences would be heaven, and we are not yet there.

A little more discussion on so-called coincidence., Consider that I mentioned my kids begging to go on the roller coaster at Kings Dominion and how if it wasn't for the thunderstorm we probably wouldn't have stopped in Lakeridge and possibly missed the meeting Father Bruse and witnessing the crying statue of Mary at the St. Elizabeth Anne Seton Church.

When I was reviewing notes and articles from our trip, I came across the following:

HOLY ENIGMA: *People.com* (*People Magazine*) by
Mary Esselman, April 27, 1992.

It's an article (one of many that probably still can be
Googled) about Father Bruse and the Crying Statue.
In it, Mary Esselman notes that Father Bruse loved
roller coasters even more than my kids. In fact, she
says, "before he entered the seminary, he set the
Guinness book's world record for roller coaster
riding." And: "The third time, he made a world record
marathon roller coaster ride—124 hours on the
Rebel Yell"—the same ride my kids were unable to
finish due to the storm! Coincidence? You tell me!

I was baptized at St. Mary's Church in East Hartford,
Connecticut. I attended St. Mary's Grammar School
and was married at St. Mary's Church in Willimantic,
Connecticut.

NOTE:

I finished the first draft of my story last night. This
morning, August 17, 2018, while having my coffee, I
watched a young female reporter, Mariana Atencio,
on MSNBC News interview a sobbing Latino
immigrant mother, who was begging to be united
with her two children who were taken from her at the
border. It was heartbreaking, and I am convinced
Mother Mary is crying for her and the rest of the
separated children and parents in New Mexico at a
church named for one of her earliest apparitions in
the Americas, at Guadalupe.

It doesn't make a lot of difference what your view on
immigration is. I'm first generation: Both parents

were immigrants. I know first-hand the problems they went through back during the Great Depression.

That conversation can be ongoing. Right *NOW* we have got to help these families reunite.

My wife and I were at a Six Flags Amusement Park thirty years ago, when my six-year-old daughter Erin went missing. I remember searching frantically.

She was lost for about a half hour. I think we were close to losing it just before she was found. (That was only one half of one hour. It seemed like an eternity.) It's hard to comprehend how these parents whose kids can't be located are managing to survive, while separated for weeks.

Think about your kids, your grandchildren, your nieces and nephews, and do something. I, and doctors, also believe the longer they're separated, the more these children could be wounded for the rest of their lives.

At the very least call your Congressmen and Senators.

Thank you for reading,
Jim Naughton

Partial list of
Mother Mary's Apparitions

It's apparent that Mary has appeared often throughout history and to many countries. Feel free to Google the history, the miracles of each:

Our Lady of Alotting, Germany 660
Our Lady of Loreto, Italy 1291
Our Lady of Siauliai, Lithuania 1457
Our Lady of Good Counsel, Genazzano, Italy 1467
Our Lady of Guadalupe, Mexico 1531
Our Lady of Ocotlan, Mexico 1541
Our Lady of Czestochowa, Poland 1655
Our Lady of Laus, France 1664
Our Lady of Peace, Santa Fe, New Mexico 1680
Our Lady of the Miraculous Medal,
         Rue du Bac, Paris, France 1830
Our Lady of La Salette, France 1846
Our Lady of Lourdes, France 1858
Our Lady of Pontmain, France 1871
Our Lady of Knock, Ireland 1879
Our Lady of Pompeii (Our Lady of the Rosary) 1884
Our Lady of Fatima, Portugal 1916
Our Lady of Beauraing, Belgium 1932
Our Lady of Banneux, Belgium 1933
Our Lady of Tears, Syracuse, Italy 1953
Our Lady of Akita, Japan 1973
Our Lady of Medjugorje 1981
Our Lady of Kibeho, Africa. 1981
Our Lady of the Redeemer, Bloomington, Indiana . . 1990
Our Lady of the Rosary of San Nicolas,
         Buenos Aires, Argentina 1983–1990
Mary Apparitions in Tensta, Sweden 2012

As stated, this is just a partial list of some of the most documented apparitions. There are many more.

News / Nation & World

A Virgin Mary statue in New Mexico has been 'weeping' olive oil. Church leaders can't explain it.

By Lindsey Bever
The Washington Post

JULY 18, 2018, 11:44 AM

Inside a Catholic church in New Mexico, a 7-foot tall bronze statue of the Virgin Mary appears to be "weeping," according to church leaders.

The sculpture, known locally as Our Lady of Guadalupe, is not crying human tears; an investigator with the Roman Catholic Diocese of Las Cruces said her "tears" have the same chemical makeup as olive oil treated with perfume - a substance that, when blessed, would be chrism, a sacred oil used in the Catholic church to anoint the parishioners. But, church leaders say, the rare occurrence has prompted people from all over to come for conversions, confessions and to watch the statue of the mother of God cry.

The question, one expert says, is not merely how it's happening (or, whether it's happening naturally) but how people are responding to the phenomenon and why they may want to believe in it.

"The Catholic church has a long history of believing in supernatural signs," John Thavis, who wrote the 2015 book "The Vatican Prophecies," said Tuesday in a phone interview. "There's a kind of curiosity and enthusiasm when something like this happens because it seems to confirm the traditional belief that God works in our own world and sometimes the supernatural is visible in our world."

USA TODAY · FRIDAY, APRIL 17, 1992 ·

OPINION USA

Why does a statue of the Virgin Mary weep?

BARBARA REYNOLDS
COLUMNIST

Mary, mother of God, why does she weep?

Tuesday night I visited a suburban church in Lake Ridge, Va., where parishioners say several statues of the Virgin Mary have wept as the Rev. James Bruse, said Mass or blessed their statues.

Bruse's wrists bare reappearing stigmata-like wounds, miracles in themselves, for they resemble the wounds of Jesus Christ on the Cross.

At opportune times, scholars say, the Virgin Mary has entered human events with miraculous results.

In 1917, in Fatima, Portugal, she prophesized the rise of Soviet tyranny and also its collapse once Russia was consecrated to her Immaculate Heart. Pope John Paul II carried out the consecration in 1984, with the fall of communism soon following. In 1981, in Medugorje, Yugostavia, after six children said the Holy Mother gave them regular messages, 10 million pilgrims visited. Many reported life-changing experiences.

Those reports, though, came from a distance, another country. But with claims of Marian miracles from California, to South Dakota, to Virginia, the epiphanies are appearing in our time, in our hour. It's as if she stands at our door and knocks.

In Kansas City, Mo, Andy Garcia runs the Medugorje book center. She hasn't traveled to Medugorje, but says the Holy Mother has traveled to her.

"I used to be a drug addict and alcoholic but quit cold turkey after I began working at the Center. I felt the Holy Mother drawing me closer, that if I trusted in Jesus, I wouldn't have to live a scum-my life."

Why does she weep?

The Holy Mother draws people away from sin and toward salvation. Her message is different for each believer. But Medugorje's message was universal, for humankind: A catastrophe overhangs our world as punishment for its neglect of God and His commandments.

At the Cross, Mary, the mother of Jesus, kept a lone vigil, while all but one of his male disciples ran away. Si entered so deeply in the pe of his suffering that pe popes had called her the C Redeemer of humanity, she weeping for all the mo ers who must also watch th sons being crucified on street corners of America?

Does she weep because t Catholic church fails to dain those of her sex to t priesthood, while calling si ism "evil"?

Does she weep because t powerful don't weep; don't a the powerless? Are we at t point where wooden statu must cry out because ser human hearts have turned stone?

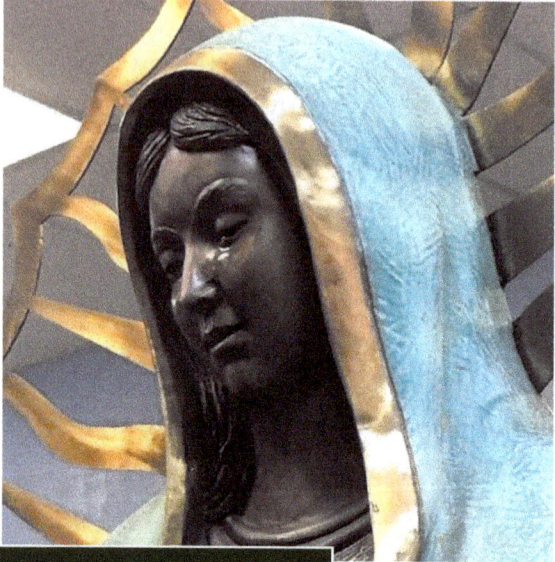

```
        Its True I tell you



Father Bruse was his name
A young man
Tall with dark brown hair
and those eyes
yes there was something mysterious
about those eyes
The way they penetrated my soul
I could feel myself drowning
in the depths of his eyes
Its true I tell you
its true
The slashes in his feet and hands
I saw it
I saw it all
The agony that Jesus went through
for him is equal
At times his wounds will open up
with discomfort and bleed
Its like a wound that can never be healed
Its true I tell you
Its true
And then the statue Virgin Mary
was crying
Through her eyes
I saw the beauty of the misty skies
People were amazed glorified
upon there knees soaking up the tears
with any cloth they could find
I saw it
I saw it all
I remember standing there in silence
seeing the expressions on my family faces
As if they were trapped between reality
and child like dreaming
Its true I tell you
Its true
Yes indeed a miracle
me and my family witnessed
I wanted to share with you that feeling I felt
That one spring day
As the cool winds of spring extinguish
a spirit stays
I saw it
I saw it all
I'm lost in a jumble of emotions
as they sweep  in and out
Its true I tell
Its true
Now I'm left with all these questions


There  are so many questions
but very little answers
For why
why is the statue spraying out her tears
and why
Why is that poor innocent man bleeding
If only I could see through walls
were reasons lies
Through his eyes I could see beauty
in the misty skies
Its true I tell you
Its true
I saw it
I saw it all
A miracle
Yes indeed
A miracle


                    By
              Erin Naughton
```

Dear Jim,   4.16.93

    Thank you so much
for your letter. I was
deeply moved by it.
Please thank Erin for
the beautiful poem about
me. I am praying for
all of you, and can sure
use your prayers.
May God bless you
many times over.

               Rev. James C. Bruse

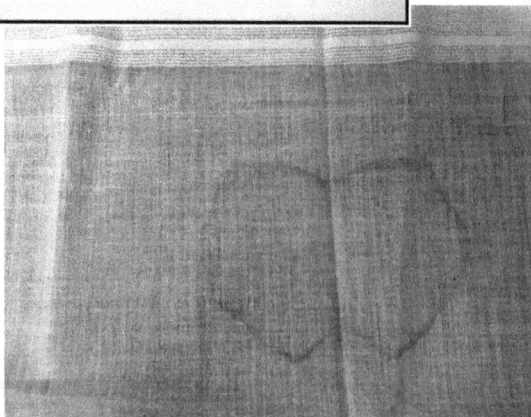

Also by James P. Naughton:

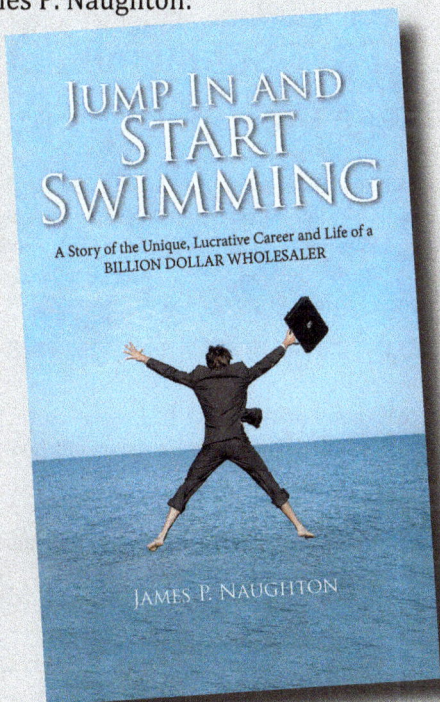

The life of a salesman isn't something one plans from the cradle. In this case, it happened after a few other things, and proceeded in directions the author didn't see coming. Billion-dollar wholesaler James P. Naughton shares his story and some plain words about the route he took to where he is today.

It may come as a surprise to many readers that one way to get to the top is simply to *jump in and start swimming.*

For purchasers of the paperback version of JUMP IN:

FREE Supplemental
College Job and Career Guide

CONTENTS INCLUDE: Applying for Jobs after College, Resumes & Cover Letters, The Interview, Contacting Companies, Suggestions for Getting a Job after Graduation, Consider the the Jobs Are, More thoughts on Websites, Resume Sample, Cover Letter Sample, Salaries for a variety of Careers)

No cost other than postage. US Postage cost = $1.50,
International =$4.09** (based on one book.)
Mail a return address and a copy of your book purchase receipt,
along with your postage check made payable to

JP NAUGHTON SALES PERFORMANCE COMPANY at:

James P. Naughton
51 Gosnold Road
North Kingstown, RI 02852

**Please email me for questions you may have or if ordering more than one guide book for postage cost for US or other.

Email - *info@keypublishingcompany.com*

More information may be found at
http://keypublishingcompany.com/supplemental-guide.html

(ebook purchasers, please refer to the web page)

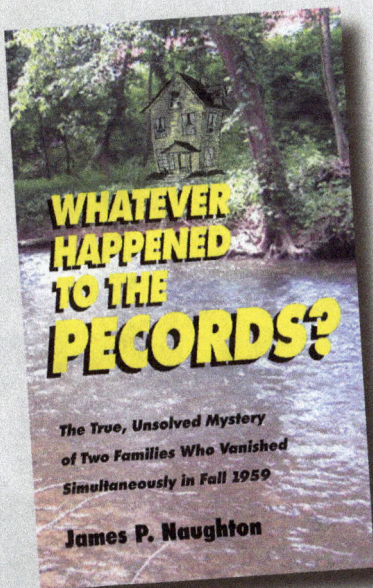

The author narrates a slide presentation on his book, *Whatever Happened to the Pecords?* (see opposite page) at Goodwin College, in East Hartford, Connecticut.

The college's location—before the college existed—figures prominently in the book, and Naughton acknowledges the kind help he received from the staff of the college when he was writing the autobiographical story.

United States Senate
WASHINGTON, D.C. 20510

March 24, 1983

Dear Mr. Naughton:

Just a line to offer my congratulations on your being named the 1982 "Man of the Year" and your selection as Associate Vice President of Dean Witter Reynolds, Incorporated.

This honor is, I am sure, well deserved and is a fine tribute to your enthusiasm and tremendously hard work.

With warm regards, renewed congratulations, and all best wishes for continued success, I am

Sincerely,

Claiborne Pell

Mr. James P. Naughton
50 Arrow Lane
North Kingstown, Rhode Island 02852

This letter marks the beginning of a multitude of acknowledgements, awards, trophies and plaques that were presented to the author over the following 30-plus years (they are included in his book, *Jump In and Start Swimming*).

www.ingramcontent.com/pod-product-compliance
Lightning Source LLC
Chambersburg PA
CBHW060643030426
42337CB00018B/3418